This Journal
Belongs to

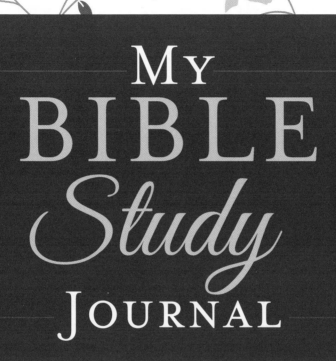

My
BIBLE
Study
JOURNAL

180 Encouraging Bible Reading for Women

DONNA K. MALTESE

BARBOUR BOOKS
An Imprint of Barbour Publishing, Inc.

Our mission is to inspire the world with the life-changing message of the Bible.

Member of the
Evangelical Christian
Publishers Association

Printed in China.

God is speaking to all of us, all the time.

The question is not, to whom does God talk?

The question is, who listens?

NEALE DONALD WALSH, AUTHOR

*W*elcome to *My Bible Study Journal*, a place where you can commune with God, His Word, and the Holy Spirit. This is your entrance into a quiet time of prayer, reading, and reflection, a way of discovering what God is speaking into your life and what He is saying to you and you alone so that you know where to go, what to do, how to think, what to say.

This journal contains six topical 30-day Bible reading plans (one page per day) to help you focus on the following areas:

Each of the 180 days covered contains that day's specific topic, scripture reading, and two to three journaling prompts.

Before beginning each day's Bible passage, *pray* for the Holy Spirit's illumination. Make it your intention to *listen* to what God is saying. Then and only then, *absorb* the Bible passage for that day.

Afterward, before looking at any commentary or considering that's day's journal-writing prompts, *mark* the verse or passage that is specifically speaking to your heart in this place and time—whether or not you understand why. Then go on to the journaling prompts. Slowly *reflect* on each one. *Respond* to the prompt that most speaks to you—or to the verse you have already marked—and see what more God may reveal. The point is to follow where God is leading. At the end of your journaling time, pray for God to embellish in your own heart, soul, and life the truths He has imparted. Ask for His strength and courage to go where the signpost has pointed.

Within these pages is your opportunity to take hold of your God, life, voice, thoughts, purpose, dreams, path, spirit, and pen. And trust you will find the path, the clue, the word to be followed.

Everything in the Scriptures is God's Word.
All of it is useful for teaching and helping people and
for correcting them and showing them how to live.
2 TIMOTHY 3:16 CEV

30 Days of Bible Readings
for Getting to Know God Better

This is what the LORD says. . .
"Those who wish to boast should boast in this alone:
that they truly know me and understand that
I am the LORD who demonstrates unfailing love."

JEREMIAH 9:23–24 NLT

*G*od is the author of the Bible, a love letter from His heart to yours. And from Genesis to Revelation, He clearly makes it known who He is and what role He will take in every area and aspect of your life.

In this first of six 30-day Bible reading plans, you will be exploring scriptures to better understand God's majesty, power, and love for you. It begins with God the Creator and ends with God the Approachable.

As you enter into your Bible reading each day, leave commentaries out of your heart-to-heart conversation with God, allowing His Word to speak for itself. Start off with a simple prayer, something like, "Here I am, Lord. Speak, Your servant is listening. I'm determined to hear what You want to tell me, to learn what You want me to know." Then read that day's scripture, intending to hear God's voice. Meditate on the reading. Underline the verse or passage that stands out to you the most. Then, and only then, expecting God to reveal Himself, read, reflect, and respond to the journal-writing prompts, being honest with yourself and God as you write. Afterward, thank God for this time together, asking Him to help you apply what you've learned to your life and heart.

God the Creator

The Spirit of God hovers over the darkness (see Genesis 1:2), the unknown, looking to create order. How might this bring you comfort?

....

....

....

....

....

What God speaks comes into being, is created. What are you speaking? What is being created in your life?

....

....

....

....

....

What does it mean to you that you have been created in the image of God, that He has blessed you, wants you to be fruitful, provides for you, and believes you are very good?

....

....

....

....

....

....

God the Sustainer

To *sustain* means to support, continue to hold up without fail. How does it feel knowing God has created all things to hold you up—including the earth beneath your feet—and continues to do so in your life today?

God formed the earthly body of Adam (meaning *earth*) from the soil but formed Eve (meaning *life*), his equal partner, not from the earth or the animal kingdom but from the rib of man himself. What does this tell you about God as a *creative* sustainer?

9

God of Promises

God talked to Abram in a vision. In what ways is He talking to you?

God told Abram not to fear—before the man even confessed that he was worried and had nothing *but* questions. How does this scenario comfort you?

On one side are God's promises that reach beyond time and space. On the other, your trust and reliance on them. Which of God's promises is He relaying to you, waiting for you to trust Him for, today?

God of Holiness

When was the last time you "took off your sandals" when meeting with God to show respect and reverence for His holiness?

In what ways do you pause in God's presence, preparing yourself—mind, body, heart, spirit, and soul—for a heavenly meeting, knowing you, the imperfect being, are approaching the perfect being?

How does your acknowledgment of God's holiness affect you—before, during, and after prayer?

God the Victor

After miraculously escaping the Egyptian pharaoh and his army, God's people sang a song of victory, saying God, their strength and their song, had become their salvation. On what occasion(s) have you come out of a battle unscathed and sung a victory song to the Lord?

....

....

....

....

....

....

....

....

What do you need to do today to tap into God's strength, assured that with Him, you need fear no enemy or flood and will, in the end, find firm footing on dry land?

....

....

....

....

....

....

....

....

God of Purity

READ EXODUS 20

Why do you think God wrote these ten commandments, which clearly point out God's purity and humankind's impurity?

....

....

....

The first four commandments are about your relationship with God, and the rest are about your relationship with others. Where might you be falling short?

....

....

....

....

....

....

What might God be pointing out to you in today's reading? What do you need to confess to draw nearer to Him?

....

....

....

....

....

....

God of Glory

Moses asks to see God's glory but could not see God's face and live. So God protected Moses by putting him in a cleft of rock and covering him with His hand as He went by. This allowed Moses to see God's back but not His face. What does this tell you of the love and care of God for His people?

....

....

....

....

....

....

....

....

In what ways do you experience God's glory in nature? In the rest of God's creation? In your life?

....

....

....

....

....

....

....

God of Blessing

God says that if you listen to and obey His voice, a myriad of blessings will come down upon you and overtake you. When have you felt God's blessings do just that because you listened to His voice?

....

....

....

....

....

....

....

God wants you to continue following His path, not turning aside to go another way. What spiritual practice have you found that keeps you in His Way? How well are you keeping to that practice? What blessings do you lose when you stray from His Way?

....

....

....

....

....

....

....

God of Judgment

In what ways do you at times forsake God, worshipping other things and people instead of Him?

....

....

....

....

When was the last time you—having done other than what God desired and feeling His judgment because of it—cried out for help?

....

....

....

....

....

In what ways, in His mercy and compassion, has God rescued you from yourself? In what ways do you think your troubles became His? How does this view—that what hurts you hurts God—change your perception of Him?

....

....

....

....

....

God the Unrivaled

What false god may be rivaling for your allegiance in your own life? What might you need to do to rebuild your altar to the Lord?

....
....
....
....
....
....

God—the One who has power over fire, water, clouds, and rain—desires the entire heart, mind, body, soul, and spirit of His people. What can you do to show Him you are wholly His?

....
....
....
....
....
....

How does it feel knowing you are the daughter of an unrivaled God?

....
....
....
....

God of Majesty

—— READ PSALM 8 ——

When was the last time you stopped and truly considered the majesty of God, the awesome works of His creation that surround you every day?

....

....

....

....

....

What range of emotions do you feel knowing that although you are just a speck in God's universe, you are also His beloved daughter, a crowned princess?

....

....

....

....

....

What things has God put into your hands and under your feet? How is His majesty reflected in these things, large and small?

....

....

....

....

....

God of Life

What words is your soul speaking to the Lord today?

....

....

....

....

....

When was the last time you asked God for advice; allowed Him to speak to your heart in the night; set Him at your right hand, knowing that with Him there you need not worry about anything because He is your protector in your life journey?

....

....

....

....

....

In what ways have you allowed God to show you the path of life and, in so doing, found joy in His presence and pleasure in eternal life with Him?

....

....

....

....

....

God of Supremacy

—— READ PSALM 19 ——

What have you witnessed in God's creation that tells you of His overwhelming supremacy over all nature?

....

....

....

....

....

In what ways does God reveal Himself and His power in your soul, thoughts, heart, and spirit?

....

....

....

....

....

In what ways have you not given God free "reign" in your life, so that your words, your actions, your thoughts, your heart, your soul, and your spirit will be pleasing to Him, the ruler of all?

....

....

....

....

....

....

God the Shepherd

PSALM 23

As you imagine God as your shepherd—the one who provides for you, gives you rest, stills your spirit, restores your soul, comforts you, guards you, and guides you—which of His provisions speaks to you the most today? Why?

....

....

....

....

....

What dark valley might you be walking through right now? What light is God shining into it?

....

....

....

....

....

How would your life change if you were conscious every moment that God the Shepherd is walking with you, is leading you, has got you covered?

....

....

....

....

....

God of Peace

In what ways do you praise and worship God before, during, and after the storms in your life? How might worshipping God *before* the storm help you endure it, to find peace amid the thunder and lightning?

What comfort does it give you knowing God is more powerful than any storm you could encounter or witness, that even in the deluge, He is still on the throne and always will be?

Where and in what situation are you craving God's strength and peace?

God of Greatness

When was the last time you praised God not for what He's done for you but because of His extreme and supreme greatness?

....

....

....

....

What person, place, or thing in your life may you have been putting on a higher pedestal than God? When you put that person, place, or thing next to God, how does it compare to His greatness?

....

....

....

....

What thoughts fill your mind as you consider that your great big God will be with you, guiding you, forever and ever?

....

....

....

....

....

God the Protector

PSALM 91

Going with the premise that the promises of Psalm 91 depend on your meeting the conditions of its first two verses, how often do you dwell in that secret place, abiding in God, acknowledging Him as your protector, and trusting Him for all?

What is God rescuing you from today? How does it feel knowing, no matter what comes against you, you are safe in His arms?

Which of the promises in this psalm are speaking most to your heart today? Why might that be?

God of Refuge

PSALM 94

In what ways do God's words, ways, and promises provide a refuge of relief for you in troubled times?

....

....

....

....

When have you cried out to God that you were falling, slipping, and His love supported you? When doubts filled your mind, in what ways did God comfort you and give you hope?

....

....

....

....

....

How does it make you feel, knowing that in times of trouble, you have a place to go? What do you do to get to that place?

....

....

....

....

....

God of Deliverance

God's mercy, faithful love, and kindness are forever. How does it feel knowing those things will follow you wherever you go?

When was the last time you called on God while you were in dire straits? How did His answer, His deliverance of you, help you find better footing?

What would happen if you began each morning knowing God is greater than anything you may face, rejoicing in the day He has made, and setting your intention to be glad in it?

God of Purpose

Isaiah 42:1-9

God supported Jesus Christ, put His Spirit upon Him, and held His hand as He opened the eyes of the blind and freed prisoners. What thoughts and feelings arise with that knowledge?

....

....

....

....

....

....

It is God who gives you breath as you stand upon the earth and spirit as you walk upon it. When do you feel this the most?

....

....

....

....

....

....

What new things is God doing in your life?

....

....

....

....

God of Forgiveness

What thoughts arise as you consider that God forgives your sins, forgets your "miss takes," not because of your character but because of His own? That, in spite of your sins, God continues to bless you in every way?

What things might you need to confess to God today, things that you may not have even confessed to yourself?

In what ways can you praise God for His amazingly generous gift of forgiving and forgetting?

God the Servant

God, the master of the universe, as Jesus, donned an apron and got down on His knees to dig out the dirt between the toes, and dry the scaly bottoms of the feet of one no better or worse than you. When was the last time you did something as servile or as humbling? How did that feel?

....

....

....

....

....

....

....

....

In what ways do you humbly yet happily serve others? What blessings have you experienced in doing so?

....

....

....

....

....

....

....

....

God of the Trinity

—— JOHN 14 ——

Jesus said that if you have seen Him, you have seen the Father. How does that change your present perception of God Himself?

Consider Jesus' saying that if you believe in Him, you will do even greater things than He did and that whatever you ask, praying in His name, you'll receive. In what ways does knowing this give you the peace Jesus promises?

The Holy Spirit has many names, such as Comforter, Helper, and Spirit of Truth. By which name do you know Him best? Why?

God the Life Giver

Jesus says that to bear fruit, you must abide or dwell in Him. For without Him, you can do nothing. How has this been tested and proved in your own life?

....

....

....

....

....

What thoughts come up when you consider you did not choose Jesus but He chose you to bear fruit and receive whatever you ask for in prayer?

....

....

....

....

....

Reflect on the fact that Jesus loves you and has sent the Holy Spirit to help guide you. In what ways does this give you life?

....

....

....

....

....

God the Savior

JOHN 19:1–37

How might this story have turned out differently if the people who played a role in ultimately executing Jesus had *really* known Him—as God the Savior?

Why might it be difficult, emotionally and spiritually, to read this account? What could make reading it easier?

Who in this story do you find hardest to identify with? The easiest to identify with? Besides Jesus, of whom are you the proudest? Of whom are you the most ashamed? What qualities might you share with each of these characters?

God of the Resurrection

MARK 16

The female followers of Jesus were the first to arrive at His tomb, ready to go about the normal duties after the death of a loved one, and were shocked to find the door of the tomb rolled away. When were you last going about your normal duties and surprised by the God of the Resurrection? Did you run away in fright and disbelief or stay to hear His message?

....

....

....

....

....

....

....

When did you first believe in the resurrected God? How is He working with you today?

....

....

....

....

....

....

....

....

God Our Friend

1 JOHN 1:1–2:14

Imagine God your friend loving you so much that He came down to earth to show you the way back to Him. You can now be a friend to Him like Eve was with Him and her fellow creature Adam before the fall. How does knowing God loves you so much help you to love and befriend your fellow creatures?

In what ways can you keep your connection to the light of God shining through you and onto others during the darkest of times?

God the Praiseworthy

In what ways do you express your praise when you look through the heavenly door standing open in your own mind and see God sitting on His throne?

....

....

....

....

....

What three aspects of God bring out the most praise from you?

....

....

....

....

Envision your prayers being in the golden bowls of incense held by heavenly creatures singing songs of praise to Jesus the Lamb. How does that make you feel? What song might you write today to express your praise to God?

....

....

....

....

....

God of Salvation

REVELATION 19

Within the first four verses of this reading, three times various heavenly creatures shout "Alleluia!" for the God of salvation, praising His victory. Consider doing so yourself, right now joining with them, then recording your thoughts and feelings—before and after your shouts of "Alleluia!"

....

....

....

....

....

....

....

....

Imagine heaven opening, revealing a white horse with a rider called Faithful and True. It's Jesus, the Son of God, who defeats all evil—saving your very life, spirit, and soul. What words of praise do you have for Him?

....

....

....

....

....

....

....

God the Approachable

Someday, you will find yourself eternally dwelling with God in a beautiful place, having a relationship with Him like Eve had before the Fall. What might be one of the first things you say or do when you see God face-to-face?

....

....

....

....

....

In what ways do you acknowledge God's presence in your everyday doings? How do you approach Him?

....

....

....

....

....

Now that you have gotten to know God better, how much more is He revealing in your life? What's the most important thing He wants you to know?

....

....

....

....

....

30 Days of Bible Readings
for Knowing Jesus Better

I want to know Christ—
yes, to know the power of his resurrection.
Philippians 3:10 NIV

*J*esus. To know Him is to love Him—and realize His love for you. From His humble earthly beginning to His spectacular supernatural never-ending, He is calling you to a purpose you can only begin to imagine.

In this second of six 30-day Bible reading plans, from Jesus' birth in the manger to His exit of the tomb, you will be exploring scriptures to better understand the Jewish leader, preacher, and teacher who forever transformed—and continues to transform—the world and the people in it.

As stated before, as you approach your Bible reading each day, remember to leave commentaries out of the conversations, allowing God's Word to speak for itself. Start off with a simple prayer, something like, "Here I am, Lord, ready to listen and learn, to hear and heed You. Let Your light shine upon me, my heart, mind, spirit, and soul." Then read that day's passage, intending to hear Jesus' voice. Meditate on the Word. Underline the verse or passage that stands out to you the most. Then, and only then, expecting Christ to reveal Himself, read, reflect, and respond to the journal-writing prompts, being honest with yourself and God as you write. Afterward, thank God for this time together, asking Him to help you apply His teachings and wisdom, His love and power, to your life and heart.

The Birth of Jesus (Part 1)

When has God stepped into your dreams and rerouted you amid one of your best-laid plans? Did you heed God's redirection or stick staunchly to your already well-laid-out path?

Have you obeyed God in a situation where He asks you to do what seems to go against tradition, public opinion, and societal norms? What was the result?

How do your expectations and God's plans differ? How do you allow room for God to speak into your life, separating your inner chatter from His divine voice?

The Birth of Jesus (Part 2)

LUKE 2:1–20

When have you discovered God's glory and richness during an ordinary life event set amid seemingly dire circumstances? What joy did that bring you?

....

....

....

....

Which unexpected happenings, things that startled you, prompted you to ponder God's amazing orchestration of life events?

....

....

....

....

How does it change your perspective, knowing that God often uses the most ordinary and lowliest of messengers to bring great goodwill and good news into the world, touching the hearts and changing the lives of others forevermore?

....

....

....

....

Visit of the Wise Men

MATTHEW 2:1–12

In what ways do you think you've had to travel far to find and worship Jesus, the King? What did your search reveal?

....

....

....

....

When was the last time you took a gift to Jesus? What was its significance to you? How do you think it was received?

....

....

....

....

....

When was the last time God warned you about something while you were dreaming or when you were in a physically, spiritually, and mentally receptive state? Were you able to allow God's counsel to override your womanly wisdom?

....

....

....

....

....

The Word Became Flesh

JOHN 1:1–28

What does it mean to you that Jesus is *the* Word who speaks all things into being and sustains all things—including you? What is Jesus speaking and sustaining in your life today?

What words or feelings come to mind when you realize that *because you believe in Jesus, you are God's daughter* and have all the birthrights and privileges that connection entails?

When have you felt like John the Baptist, a lone voice crying in the wilderness?

A Light Has Risen

When have you felt as if you were being swallowed up by darkness? What were you thinking and feeling at the time? How did you get back into the light?

Where do you go when you are discouraged, when those you love are imprisoned spiritually, emotionally, mentally, or physically? How or why does that place soothe you?

What are some of the Bible verses you rely on to keep you from being overcome by the darkness? How does the Word keep you in the light?

Jesus' Ministry in Galilee

LUKE 4:14—37

Is it your custom, as it was Jesus' (see Luke 4:16), to go to church every Sabbath? Why or why not?

....

....

....

....

....

When, if ever, have you gone "home" and been treated with disdain by the people there because of your faith? Were you able to pass through their midst and go on your way? What gave you the power to do so?

....

....

....

....

....

In what situations has Jesus come and healed your broken heart? Liberated your imprisoned spirit? Given your mind new insight? Set your soul free from oppression?

....

....

....

....

....

Jesus' True Family

Jesus calls to Himself those He wants to work with Him. When did Jesus call you? How has your life changed as a result?

To what has Jesus called you to work with Him? How do you tap into His power to fulfill that calling?

Those who do God's will are Jesus' brother, sister, and mother. How does it feel to claim that privilege? How would your life perspective change if you keep your role as His sister or mother uppermost in your thoughts?

Jesus Cleanses the Temple
and Meets with Nicodemus

JOHN 2:12–3:21

In what ways have you given material things and mental "transactions" priority over prayer and worship within your own temple of God?

What thoughts and feelings come to the fore when you realize that Jesus knows exactly what is in your heart and mind?

What changes occurred in your life after your spirit was born of God's Spirit? How do you nourish the "new you"?

Parables of Jesus

Which of these parables is speaking most to your soul today? Why might that be?

....

....

....

....

....

In what ways do you prepare the ground of your heart so that when the seed of God's Word falls on it, you are able to readily accept it and bear fruit because of it?

....

....

....

....

....

How does it encourage you knowing that the more you think and study about what you read in God's Word, the more wisdom you will get out of it? How has that already been proved in your life?

....

....

....

....

....

The Heart of Humankind

MARK 7

When might you have found yourself praising Jesus with your lips while your heart was far removed from Him? What feelings and thoughts come to mind when you consider that when your heart is aligned with Jesus', there is no physical distance He cannot breach to answer your prayer?

....

....

....

....

....

What are you persistently praying about these days? How might God be using this prayer experience to test your faith?

....

....

....

....

....

What is Jesus commanding your heart to be opened to today?

....

....

....

....

....

Equality with God

Although angels may stir healing waters into which you may walk, it is Jesus who, knowing you inside out, performs the whole healing. How might this change the spiritual order of things in your mind?

....

....

....

....

....

Which more closely describes you: a follower of the rules or a follower of the Rule Maker? Which do you think is the better of the two?

....

....

....

....

....

Because you have heard Jesus' words and believe God sent Him, you have eternal life. What thoughts and feelings does this fact inspire?

....

....

....

....

....

Sermon on the Mount (Part 1)

MATTHEW 5

Which of the "Blessed are" statements (see Matthew 5:3–10) apply to you today? How does that comfort or strengthen you?

In what ways are you letting your light shine so that your good works can point others to God?

Who is Jesus prompting you to forgive today? For whom are you to go the second mile? Which enemy is He prompting you to bless? How does it feel to follow through on Jesus' promptings? How might it become a habit for you to follow Jesus' nudges every day?

Sermon on the Mount (Part 2)

MATTHEW 6

What behind-the-scenes do-good deed can you perform for someone in your life, a deed that you keep just between you and God? After following through, what reward did you openly receive from God as a result?

....

....

....

....

....

Where is your secret prayer closet? What is it like? How often do you use it?

....

....

....

....

How does seeking first the Kingdom of God help you forgive others, lay up treasures in heaven instead of on earth, keep you loyal to God instead of money, and stave off worrying about tomorrow?

....

....

....

....

....

Sermon on the Mount (Part 3)

MATTHEW 7

What would your thoughts and words be like if you refrained from judging others? How might your doing so draw others closer to God?

Only as you continually ask, seek, and knock will you receive, find, and have doors opened. How might keeping this in mind every day help you live a fuller life with God?

How would your life change if you treated everyone—regardless of who they are or what they have done—just as *you* would want to be treated twenty-four hours a day?

Power over the Physical World

How does the fact that Jesus has the power to still the winds and waves calm you? How does the idea that Jesus is *always* in your boat help you face life's trials?

....

....

....

....

....

When have you felt the power of Jesus stanching the flow of issues in your life? How has knowing that your faith has made you well bring you joy and peace?

....

....

....

....

....

What power do the words "Don't be afraid; only believe" hold for you? How would life change if they were your mantra?

....

....

....

....

....

Power to Heal (Part 1)

MATTHEW 8:1–17

When asking Jesus for healing, how are you like (or unlike) the leper who came to Him, worshipped Him, and then stated his faith by saying he knew Jesus could heal him if He was willing?

Nothing impedes Jesus' healing power—neither time nor distance. What does that tell you about Jesus' role, presence, and power in your life?

How does it feel knowing Jesus doesn't just heal you and those you love but actually takes all illnesses and injuries upon Himself?

Power to Heal (Part 2)

What signs and wonders has Jesus performed that have helped you to believe in Him?

A certain nobleman heard Jesus say his son would live, put his trust in that fact, and then went on his way assured it was true. When have you heard Jesus' Word, trusted in Him and it, and went away, assured of His truth? What miracle did you uncover because you heard, trusted, and were assured?

Loving the Unlovely

—— Luke 5:12–26 ——

Has there ever been a time when you've fallen onto your face, stated your faith, and then simply and humbly awaited Jesus' response and touch? How different is that than just telling Jesus what you want Him to do?

....
....
....
....
....

What do you do or where do you go to recharge spiritually, physically, emotionally, and mentally?

....
....
....
....
....

What do you do when the unlovely, unclean, and undesirable approach? Do you willingly put out your hand and touch them with the love of Jesus? If not, what might help you do so?

....
....
....
....

The Cost of Discipleship

Do you desire to go after Jesus, or do you shy away from His trail?
Do you deny yourself or deny Him? Do you take up your cross or
leave it on the ground?

What does it mean to you when Jesus says that if you want to save your
life, you'll lose it; but if you lose your life for Him, you'll save it?

What might you be putting before God? What might you have gained
lately at the expense of your soul?

Who Is the Greatest?

LUKE 9:46–62

What are the ways in which you may be seeking to make a name for yourself rather than a name for Jesus?

....

....

....

....

....

When was the last time you steeled yourself to face something difficult? How might what you're learning about Jesus help you in future challenges?

....

....

....

....

....

What steps can you take to keep yourself looking forward instead of backward in your faith walk? What affirming Bible verses might help you in this endeavor?

....

....

....

....

....

Greatness in the Kingdom

MATTHEW 18

Which verse in this chapter struck the loudest chord in your heart? In what ways does that verse connect to the present circumstances of your life?

How does humbleness play a part in each of the vignettes presented in this chapter? In what ways does this make you stop and take stock of yourself?

Whom do you find yourself forgiving over and over again? Whom do you need to forgive *from the heart* today?

True Riches

In what ways have you accepted Jesus and received the Kingdom of God as a little child would? How have you continued to have the unyielding and total faith of a child?

Where are your treasures residing lately—in heaven or on earth? What are those treasures? In answering these questions, what insights are you gleaning about your life?

In what ways is God giving you the means and motivation to put Him before all earthly treasures? How is He making what seems impossible, possible?

Healing on the Sabbath

In what ways was Jesus a rebel? In what ways does He *continue* to be a rebel?

In what ways was Jesus a rebel? In what ways does He *continue* to be a rebel?

What weight has been bending you over lately? What or who do you need to raise yourself up? What or who do you need to get straight?

In what instances might you, daughter of Abraham, be blindly following some rules instead of following the promptings of Jesus? What might He be telling you or leading you to?

Sign of Jonah

MATTHEW 12:22–45

What is your fruit? What is it revealing about you to you? To others? To Jesus?

How are your words saving you? How might they be damning you? How might the fact that your words carry so much power affect your speech in the future? How might that fact affect your thoughts in the future?

When have you asked God for a sign instead of relying on your faith? What prompted you to do so? What was the result?

Anointing at Bethany

In what ways do you believe you have done what you could for Jesus? What more might Jesus be prompting you to do for Him?

When has Jesus prompted you to do something others scorned as a waste of time and money? Did you find yourself responding to Jesus' request or were you swayed into inaction by the naysayers? What was the result?

How would Jesus have you respond to critics—believers and nonbelievers alike—when you follow through with what God would have you do?

Institution of the Lord's Supper

MARK 14:12–31

How does it increase your faith, knowing Jesus knows all that is going to greet you in every step of your walk with Him?

....

....

....

....

....

How does the knowledge that Jesus deeply desires you to take communion in remembrance of Him keep the ritual from becoming routine?

....

....

....

....

When have you broken a solemn pledge to Jesus—despite your determination to keep it? Jesus not only later forgave Peter but used him greatly to further the Kingdom. What does this tell you about your Savior?

....

....

....

....

....

Betrayal and Arrest of Jesus

In what ways do you think you may be following Jesus at a distance? How might that affect how nonbelievers see you? How might it affect you?

....

....

....

....

....

In what situations have you been as meek and quiet as a lamb, knowing that's how God wanted you to be? When have you not been able to contain yourself? What does the fact that Jesus kept His cool reveal about Him?

....

....

....

....

....

When have you gone the way of the crowd instead of the way of God?

....

....

....

....

....

Death of Jesus

How do you think Jesus, who had all the power, felt about being presumed and mocked as powerless? Have you ever had the same type of experience?

When have you, innocent as a lamb, been betrayed by a friend, falsely accused, punished, mocked, cursed, and felt God had left you high and dry? How does it feel knowing Jesus suffered all that—and more—*for you*? What does that reveal to you about God? About Jesus?

Jesus Is Buried

In what ways have you kept your faith in Jesus secret or under cover of darkness for fear of the comments or actions of others? How might it feel to own up to your faith, to step into the light, to take action for Jesus by serving Him before others in some way?

What do you think about the fact that the fall of humanity happened in a garden and that the rise of humanity also took place in a garden?

The Tomb Is Empty

JOHN 20:1–18

When was the last time you ran to Jesus, eager to see the One who calls you "dear woman"? Where do you usually find Him?

....

....

....

....

When have you seen—and then believed? In what ways does Jesus bless you for believing in Him even though you have not yet physically seen Him? What helps you keep that faith strong?

....

....

....

....

....

What about scripture is still hard for you to understand? What about the scriptures has Jesus made clear to you? What is He revealing to you?

....

....

....

....

....

30 Days of Bible Readings
for Growing in Your Faith

*[Urged on] by faith Abraham, when he was called, obeyed and went
forth to a place which he was destined to receive as an inheritance;
and he went, although he did not know or trouble
his mind about where he was to go.*

HEBREWS 11:8 AMPC

The more you grow your faith, the stronger your relationship with God will become. The stronger your relationship, the more in tune you will be with the one who will lead you to wonderful places, places you never dreamed of or began to imagine. The more courage you will have to walk where He wants you to walk, to do what He has called you to do. And you will find yourself doing it with ease and peace of mind and heart.

The great adventure begins and ends in the Word. In the next 30 days, you will be growing your faith by soaking in God's truth, allowing it to become part of your very being. Soon you will find yourself being prompted, actuated, and urged on by faith, waiting confidently and looking expectantly for what God will have you do next.

Approach the Word with reverence, read the scripture, and intend to hear God speak and the Spirit translate. Meditate on what you've read; underline the passage that stands out the most. Then read, reflect on, and respond to the journal-writing prompts, knowing God will lead you where He intends you to go.

Faith: Trusting God with Everything

GENESIS 22:1–14

Write about a time when you have obeyed God without question or hesitation. What was at stake? How did that experience confirm and strengthen your faith?

....

....

....

....

When has God provided *for* you in the midst of your offering that which He has demanded *from* you? How did that grow your faith and trust in Him?

....

....

....

....

....

....

What current situation in your life is testing your faith and obedience to God? What do you think you may have to sacrifice?

....

....

....

....

....

Faith: Trusting God through Prayer

1 SAMUEL 1:7–20

When have you gone to the Lord with a broken heart, crying bitter tears and pouring out your soul to Him in prayer, trusting in His compassion? How did you feel afterward?

....

....

....

....

....

Have you kept the vows you have made to God, being faithful to the part you have promised to play in your relationship with Him?

....

....

....

....

How do you prayerfully approach God—from the heart or from the head? Do you rise with a peaceful or preoccupied countenance?

....

....

....

....

....

Faith: Trusting God for Protection

In difficult circumstances, you may find yourself looking around instead of up. What can you do to keep your eyes focused on your heavenly God?

When have you sang praises to God, confident He would look out for, protect, and bless you, in the midst of a seemingly hopeless and potentially dangerous situation? How did that attitude and outlook help see you through?

What do you have to sing praises to God about today?

Faith: Trusting God to the End

What false idol might you have trusted and worshipped more than God? What came of this misdirected faith and adoration?

When have you proclaimed you would have faith and trust in God, worshipping and serving Him—regardless of whether He saved you from an undesirable end?

God walks with you amid fiery situations, leaving you unsinged spiritually, physically, emotionally, mentally, and financially. How does that truth grow your faith even more?

Faith in His Power

MATTHEW 8:1–13; 15:21–28

Have you, while worshipping Jesus, told Him that, if He is willing, He *has* the power to heal you? How might this be more of a faith booster than telling Him *how* you'd like Him to heal you?

Jesus' healing touch can reach beyond time and distance. How has that proved true in your life or the lives of those you love?

How persistent are you in crying out to Jesus, worshipping Him, requesting He heal someone you love? How has doing so changed you?

Faith in His Touch

When has your persistent, doggedly determined, against-all-odds faith prompted you to reach out to touch Jesus and made you well—spiritually, physically, emotionally, or mentally?

....

....

....

....

....

What happens to you in your life depends on the faith you have in Jesus' abilities and power to touch and change you and, at times, your circumstances. What proof have you seen of this in your life?

....

....

....

....

....

What touch do you need from Jesus today?

....

....

....

....

....

Faith in Action

When have your needs and desperation driven you to your knees before Jesus? What remedy did you request? What part did your faith play?

....

....

....

....

....

Regardless of your amount of faith in a particular area or circumstance, all things are possible with God. How has that fact boosted your faith enough to take action against all odds?

....

....

....

....

....

In what areas of your life do your doubts erode your faith? What can you do to shore up that faith?

....

....

....

....

....

Faith Grows

In what ways do you nourish your fledgling faith so that it not only grows but takes flight? What role do God, Jesus, and the Holy Spirit play in your spiritual nurturing?

....

....

....

....

How do you wait on the Lord with confidence and hopeful expectation? How does doing so increase strength you may not realize you have?

....

....

....

....

God would rather you approach Him like a divine child to a heavenly father than a petitioner to an authority figure. Which is rooted in love? Which is more effective?

....

....

....

....

Faith in God's Glory

John 7:38–39; 20:24–31

Through Jesus, God provides supernatural water for spiritually parched people. In what ways do you thirst for God? How do you satisfy that thirst?

Once relieved of spiritual thirst, are you a refreshing conduit of the Holy Spirit, allowing His rejuvenating waters to flow through you and into others?

In what areas of your life do you give more weight and credence to what you can see rather than what you believe? How might Jesus be prompting you to believe and be blessed?

Faith Is Intentional

When God's message is heard, faith grows. Are you intentionally listening to God when He speaks, or are you distracted by the noise of the world?

....

....

....

....

....

In what ways might God be stretching out His hands to you but you, not even looking for Him, cannot see them?

....

....

....

....

....

How might your life change and your faith grow if you intentionally sought God's face and presence? What if you listened alertly, were all ears, waiting for Him to speak, to understand His words and meaning?

....

....

....

....

....

Faith through Your Doubts

GALATIANS 3:1–14

Spiritual strength is more pleasing to God than human effort. Do you strain to please Him through physical works or by soaking in His Word, coming to Him in prayer, allowing His Spirit to fill you, following wherever He leads?

How do you keep the Gospel fresh in your mind and a cornerstone of your faith? How does that stave off any doubts that might creep in?

Are you a daughter of Abraham, trusting and relying on God, stepping out even though you don't know what lies ahead?

Faith Despite the Fight

Faith changes your values. What in your life has become increasingly less important as you continue your faith walk? What has become more important?

....

....

....

....

....

What are you striving for—following a bunch of holy rules or getting to know Christ intimately? Which makes you stronger and fiercer in your spiritual journey?

....

....

....

....

....

What might it feel like to get so close to Christ that you experience His resurrection power? How close are you to doing so?

....

....

....

....

....

Faith to Approach God

HEBREWS 4:16; 10:19—25

Jesus has been through it all and seen it all. How does that knowledge give you the boldness to walk right up to Him and ask for help, understanding, and compassion? What else are you in need of that He is more than ready to give?

Now that Jesus has opened the doorway to God, how confident are you that you are presentable to Him? That He will keep His promises and never go back on His word?

Faith in Our Future Home

When your Creator God spoke, He made visible things appear out of the invisible. In what ways does God's Word continue to fashion your world?

....

....

....

....

....

The Bible contains amazing examples of historical faith walkers. How does this list boost your faith? Who do you most identify with?

....

....

....

....

In what ways do invisible things—such as air and gravity—confirm your belief in God, Jesus, and the Holy Spirit? How do you draw near to an invisible God? How does He reward you, an earnest and diligent seeker?

....

....

....

....

Faith Drives Good Works

JAMES 2:14–26

Your faith is revealed by your actions. What good works does your faith prompt you to perform? How are you satisfying those urgings? Have you asked God to approve the work of your hands?

Who can you help today? What actions can you take to alleviate someone's suffering, directly or indirectly, openly or covertly?

How are your actions, your works, making your faith complete? How are your works alone showing others you are right with God?

Faith in the Spirit

Jesus left behind the Holy Spirit to help you live, love, and serve God and His people. What words of praise do you have for the Helper and Comforter?

How is the Holy Spirit guiding you? What truths is He revealing to you?

Which of the Holy Spirit's roles—Comforter, Counselor, Strength-ener, Standby, Advocate, Intercessor, etc.—is He playing most predominantly in your life right now?

Faith in the Final Outcome

Jesus' sacrifice entitles you to eternal life with God. How is He, your ultimate Savior, showing up in your life?

As a believer in Jesus, you are considered born of God, *and* your faith gives you victory over the world. In what ways are you, daughter of God, triumphing in your life?

How does your perspective change when you realize that, because of your faith in Jesus, you are already living the life eternal?

Obedience to His Commandments

Who do you think Jesus may have found difficult to love? Who do *you* find it difficult to love? In what ways can you love that person with the love of Jesus?

Jesus commands you to love as He loved and to walk as He walked. How does your doing so not only grow your faith but also demonstrate your love for Him?

How does your staying faithful to the teachings of Christ keep you closely tied to both Christ your Brother and God your Father?

Obedience Trumps Sacrifice

When have you prided yourself on following God's promptings only to later realize you'd fallen short of all He'd wanted you to do?

Why might you only hear (or listen to) half of what God says? What can you do to ensure you're giving God your total attention so that you can be wholly obedient?

God views your obedience and submission as being more valuable to Him than any sacrifice or offering you could make. Where do you need to obey and submit to Him today?

Obedience Honors His Holiness

Your obedience to God's Word, will, and way keeps you on the *righteous* track. How does such submission result in your joy and God's pleasure?

How can you keep your whole heart seeking after God? What can you do to keep your spiritual appetite whetted and fulfilled?

When might you have felt you were far from where God wanted you to be? What in God's Word inspires you to keep on following Him, to celebrate faith-walk milestones?

Obedience Leads to Righteousness

DEUTERONOMY 6; ROMANS 2:1–16

In what ways does obeying God's commands and worshipping *only* *Him* keep you in the land flowing with milk and honey?

Snuggle up to God, telling Him you love Him with all your heart, soul, and strength. Record your thoughts and feelings. How might practicing this exercise keep you on the right path with God—and lead others to follow?

How does recalling all God has done for you keep your faith strong and your walk sure?

Obedience, Because of Deliverance

What do you feel you may have left behind so that you could focus more on what God has been calling you to do? What is/was your reward for faithfully following as commanded?

God wants you to love and serve Him with all your heart and soul. How does doing so help you to obey all His commands and to gain an unwavering grip on Him?

Obedience to the One Who Sustains

JOHN 15:1–17

When you abide in Jesus the Vine, His sap flows through you, energizing, nourishing, and loving you. What steps do you take daily to keep yourself abiding in Jesus?

....

....

....

....

....

How does obedience become a natural thing to one who abides in Jesus the Vine, tended by God the Gardner? How much easier to bear fruit, to ask and receive?

....

....

....

....

....

Jesus chose you, to live in, love, and save you. How does that knowledge make it easy for you to love Him and others in return?

....

....

....

....

....

Obedience Brings Strength

LUKE 6:46—49; ACTS 4:18—21

Jesus wants you to come to Him, listen to what He is teaching you, and then *obey* that teaching. How do those three steps shore up your faith?

....

....

....

....

....

In what areas of your life might you be calling Jesus "Lord" but not following through with what He wants you to do?

....

....

....

....

....

When has your faith and obedience given you the strength to do and say what God has called you to do and say, even though it meant going against the crowd or authorities?

....

....

....

....

....

Obedience to Truth

PSALM 1; ACTS 5:28–32

God's Word holds gems of wisdom that can help direct you and your life. What would happen if you made it your daily intent to look with delight for such treasures of truth? What jewel have you found today?

How does meditating on the truth of God's Word and then *obeying* it not only nourish but prosper you in your life?

How does knowing you have the Holy Spirit, the harbinger of all truth, living within you make you more confident?

Obedience without Question

Abram stepped out in faith, obeying without question, not knowing where he was headed. When have you done the same? How did God bless your obedience? What miracles did He perform?

Where might God be calling you to step out now? What armies or obstacles may be keeping you from stepping out in faith?

How does it feel knowing that, even though you may for some time wander in a wilderness, God will take care of you because you obeyed without question?

Obedience Yields Blessings

— Leviticus 26:1–13; Psalm 119:56–62; James 2:10–13 —

Your worship of God alone and your obedience to His will and way lead to blessings. How has this been proved in your life?

Think about where you have been walking lately. What detours may you have made from God's path? Where do you need to turn to get back on the right track, following the route God would have you take?

What little amount of disobedience to God might be causing you to trip up completely?

Obedience Matters

When has your disobedience to God resulted in less than pleasant circumstances in your life?

. . . .

. . . .

. . . .

. . . .

If you are feeling dissonance between yourself and God, take some time to reflect. What might God have been asking you to do or say, or where might He have been asking you to go?

. . . .

. . . .

. . . .

. . . .

. . . .

You show your love to Jesus by following His words and teachings. How does the Holy Spirit help you to do so?

. . . .

. . . .

. . . .

. . . .

. . . .

Growth through His Promises

God urges you to, in faith, obey Him, listening to Him, doing all He asks. When you do, He then performs His promises. What are you hearing God speak into your life today? What are you obeying—or disobeying? What promises is He coming through on?

In what ways do God's promises grow you up in faith, helping you to turn your back on the less-than-perfect world and drawing you closer to the wonders of a life with God?

Growth through His Likeness

God wants you to imitate Him, following in His footsteps, like Father, like daughter. In what ways is His resemblance growing in you?

What of your old self/life may be trying to call you back into that former world? What of your new self/life is calling you forward, into the world of God? How might you grow your faith to keep you in God's realm?

How is your love for God, yourself, and others making you more like Christ?

30 Days of Bible Readings
with Great Women of Scripture

---

*Who knows but that you have come to the kingdom for
such a time as this and for this very occasion?*
ESTHER 4:14 AMPC

The Bible contains many stories of heroines. Each female's tale gives you insight into how a particular woman related to God—and how God related to her. It shows you the world she lived in, how she viewed it and her family, how she lived her life, and how she dealt with trials and triumphs. In the 30 days that follow, beginning with Eve and ending with Priscilla, make it your intention to discover what God may be speaking into your life. Consider how your own life story may compare to that of a woman who lived thousands of years ago.

As with all the other Bible reading plans, please allow God's Word to speak for itself. Pray before reading the passages, and then read that day's scripture with the intention of honing in on God's commentary only. Meditate on what you have read. Then underline the verse or verses that the Spirit directs you to. Next, read, reflect, and respond to each journaling prompt, keeping the conversation between you and God, being honest with yourself and Him. Afterward, say a prayer of thanks for the insights you have gleaned, and request His strength and power to apply what you have learned to your life, heart, body, soul, spirit, and mind.

Eve

Your ancestress Eve, the mother of all the living, was lured away from God's order and voice by the wrong desires of her heart, the urge to possess something, and the craving of her own ego. When has this happened to you?

When have you twisted what God has said to fit a need you want fulfilled? What was the result?

When have you tried to hide yourself or your deed from God? Did you end up playing the blame game or come clean and ask God for forgiveness?

Sarah

GENESIS 18:1–15; 21:1–7

What once seemingly impossible thing has God made possible in your life, exactly as promised, that brought you joy and laughter?

Sarah laughed to herself, believing God could never perform a certain promise in her life. Have you? Has God ever called you on it? Do you really believe, in your heart of hearts, that anything is too hard for the Lord?

What promise are you wanting God to fulfill in your life today? What if He will, if you would only ask?

Miriam

Miriam stood at a distance, watching and waiting to see what God would do. When have you done the same? What kept you vigilant and confident God would work?

What helps you to come out from behind the reeds, approach a potentially perilous situation, and speak what God would have you speak?

In what ways do you lead other faithful females? What song would God have you sing in celebration of Him and His deeds?

Zipporah

Although Zipporah's story is short, her boldness and determination played a great role. When have you played a small part in someone's story that either saved her in some way or led her to great things?

....

....

....

....

What bold action might God be asking you to take to help someone else fulfill her calling? What bold actions have others taken to help you fulfill your own?

....

....

....

....

....

How might boldness and determination help you willingly be steered into danger or uprooted for a place unknown to further God's Kingdom?

....

....

....

....

Rahab (Part 1)

JOSHUA 2

Rahab disobeyed a human authority or law in order to obey God or His divine law. When might you have done the same? What were the results of going with God instead of man?

....

....

....

....

What miracle work of God convinced you He is real, the supreme God to be worshipped, obeyed, and followed? What personal experience of God's work in your own life convinced you even further?

....

....

....

....

....

How good are you at following the instructions of God's "scouts"? How readily do you accept their terms?

....

....

....

....

....

....

Rahab (Part 2)

Rahab and her family were spared because, at the risk of her life, she followed the promptings of her heart for God. Where in your life might you benefit by following Rahab's example?

....

....

....

....

....

To what lengths has God gone in your own life to make good on His promise(s) to you?

....

....

....

....

....

When has your standing apart from the home crowd and going against societal rules led you to be rewarded not only with protection but with a new life?

....

....

....

....

....

Deborah and Jael (Part 1)

Deborah was wise, courageous, and just. Jael had cunning and boldness. In what ways might you display the same attributes as these women?

....

....

....

....

In what situations have you felt impelled or been prompted by God to be the real strength and support behind the man (or woman) leading an endeavor against all odds?

....

....

....

....

When have you ever stepped away from your family's defined roles and stood up for God and His people? What was the result?

....

....

....

....

....

Deborah and Jael (Part 2)

JUDGES 5

If you wrote a victory song to the Lord for what He has done in your life, what might the lyrics be?

....

....

....

....

In what ways have you arisen as a mother for God's people? What spiritual habits/routines gave you the strength and courage to do so? What kept you risen?

....

....

....

....

....

Two seemingly ordinary women in love with God, rose up in power and, by a single brave act, turned the tide to victory for God and His people. Where is God prompting you to rise up?

....

....

....

....

....

....

Ruth (Part 1)

Ruth's determination, persistence, and selflessness led her to great things. When have you persisted in sticking to someone or something, refusing to turn back? What prompted you? What role did God play?

In what situations have acts of kindness only led you so far before you turned around and went back to the familiar?

What blessings might you find in going more than the extra mile for someone who is alone and abandoned, bitter and bereft? How might God reward you?

Ruth (Part 2)

RUTH 2

Ruth fell at Boaz's feet in gratitude for his treatment of her. When was the last time you exuberantly thanked someone for his or her kindness, wondering what you did to deserve it? What was that person's response?

In what ways have you stepped into a strange, new area and taken refuge under God's wings? How has your consciousness of God's refuge kept you strong and hopeful?

Kindness often breeds more kindness, faithfulness more faithfulness. To whom can you show kindness today? To whom can you be faithful?

Ruth (Part 3)

Ruth set her cap for Boaz instead of a young wealthy man. In what ways have you eschewed the glitz and glamour and gone for the godly and good? How did that work out?

....

....

....

....

....

With what does God fill your hands and life that He wants you to share with others? With whom can you share your blessings?

....

....

....

....

How do you maintain your patience when you're waiting for the results of someone else's actions? What Bible verses might you rely on to keep you from impatiently tapping your foot?

....

....

....

....

....

....

Ruth (Part 4)

RUTH 4

Ruth went way beyond the call of duty to remain loyal to Naomi. When have you done the same? What prompted you to do so—God or public opinion? In what ways did your selfless deed lead to blessings beyond all you ever hoped or imagined?

....

....

....

....

....

....

....

When has your work for someone else prompted others to praise that person instead of you? How did you feel when you saw that person get the public acclamations? What reward did you receive?

....

....

....

....

....

....

....

Hannah (Part 1)

In what ways, if ever, have you been taunted for a perceived lack of something? How did you react and respond?

Hannah's husband loved her just as she was. Who has loved you for you—just as you are? How did or does that feel? Who do you love just as they are? How do you think God loves you?

When was the last time you gave a much-desired blessing back to God? What blessing can you give back to Him today?

Hannah (Part 2)

Hannah said God made her strong. To whom or what do you attribute your strength? Why do Hannah's lyrics say no one will make it by muscles alone?

In what ways do you accept good from the Lord? In what ways do you accept the not-so-good from Him? What would your life be like if you worshipped God from a joyful heart regardless of what you receive?

How might you be continuing to nurture your gift to God? How does He bless you repeatedly because of it?

Abigail

When have you quickly yet covertly stepped into a situation and then humbled yourself in an attempt to avert disaster? What was the result of your intercession? In what ways do you think it was God who urged you to intercede? How did God reward you for obeying His promptings?

....

....

....

....

....

....

....

....

Abigail's husband, the ungodly Nabal, is described as wicked, crude, ill-tempered, mean, and a fool. How would you describe Abigail? To which of her godly qualities might God be prompting you to aspire?

....

....

....

....

....

....

....

Esther (Part 1)

ESTHER 1:1—2:18

When have you seen choices made in anger backfire? How might anger deviate God's people from His plan?

....

....

....

....

Esther was advised to keep her background a secret. In what ways might you be keeping secrets from others? How might doing so be creating dissonance in your life or with God? How might it be protecting you from perceived harm?

....

....

....

....

....

When have you felt you were just one of many? How does it feel knowing *God* views you as singularly precious and the queen of His heart?

....

....

....

....

....

Esther (Part 2)

When, if ever, has your refusal to respect someone or something led to retribution against you? How did God use the circumstances to His or your benefit?

....

....

....

....

....

In what ways do God's laws and Christ's teachings differ from those followed by the rest of the world?

....

....

....

....

Consider the idea that maybe you were made by God to live in this place and time for a specific reason, purpose, or duty. What might that reason, purpose, or duty be?

....

....

....

....

....

Esther (Part 3)

ESTHER 5

Esther prayed and fasted before taking a daring step. When has something so significant occurred in your life that you prayed and fasted before acting? How did doing so aid you?

....

....

....

....

....

When have you used peaceable means to divert threatened violence directed at yourself or others? How did responding calmly instead of angrily give God room to work? What was the result?

....

....

....

....

When have you let one disappointing situation overshadow the joy and appreciation of all the blessings surrounding you? How might that have led you into momentary defeat?

....

....

....

....

Esther (Part 4)

Your and others' obedience to God can have a domino effect. When has someone else's obedience to God's prompting aided you in *your* plans? In what ways might that make you more willing to obey God's urgings in your own life?

....

....

....

....

....

....

....

When has your pride and ego led to you down an unbelievably unpleasant and unforeseen path of humiliation? How might God have let that happen to bring you back to Him, His will, His way, and His purpose for you?

....

....

....

....

....

....

....

Esther (Part 5)

Esther's humbleness eventually led to great acclaim. Has that ever happened to you?

When has your despair led you to take an inappropriate action, which resulted in even more trouble? What Bible verses might bring you peace and comfort amid despair then help lift you up out of the pit to a place of surer footing with God?

When, if ever, have your imagined vengeance and judgment for someone else fallen on your own head? How might that prove the benefits of following Jesus' edict to love your enemies?

Esther (Part 6)

When has something once used for evil been used for your good? What does this suggest to you about God's overall plan for your life?

....

....

....

....

Once Esther had gained her initial boldness, it continued to grow in her. How has the idea that the performance of one act of courage strengthens you to do more acts of courage been proved in your own life?

....

....

....

....

....

When has God turned your angst into blessing, your fear into fortune, your discouragement into delight, your worry into wonder?

....

....

....

....

....

Esther (Part 7)

Because of the godly Esther, Haman's best-laid human plans led to his own downfall. When has the exact opposite of what you thought would happen happened? How did God use that to increase your faith and further His Kingdom?

When have you seen people reaping what they have sown, getting what they deserve? In what ways has this spiritual law affected your own life?

How has God turned your sorrow into gladness, your mourning into joy? How do you celebrate and commemorate those events?

The Virtuous Woman

Some scholars believe the Virtuous Woman of Proverbs 31 is a personification of wisdom, a summing up of all the attributes of wisdom contained in the book of Proverbs. How might your perception of the Virtuous Woman and yourself change when you read this chapter in such a light?

Charisma is misleading and beauty doesn't last forever, but a woman who reverently fears God will be much praised. How does that truth lead you to aspire to be less of a worldly Wonder Woman and more of a wise Woman of the Way?

Elizabeth

LUKE 1:5–25, 39–45, 57–66

God had heard Zechariah's prayers for Elizabeth's bearing a child. When did someone else's prayers bring a joyful miracle into your own life? How does that encourage you to pray for others?

Although Zechariah and Elizabeth were obedient to God, Zechariah doubted God's ability to do what He promised. How might your doubts—spoken or unspoken—build obstacles in your life? How might God be getting around you and your misgivings to come through with blessings? What can you do to break down any current obstacle-creating doubts?

Mary

When filled with confusion and doubt, how does God's voice, His words of "Don't be afraid; you're the apple of My eye," break into your thoughts and boost your faith?

....

....

....

....

Mary told God she was His servant, ready, willing, and able for Him to use her as He would. How might your attitude and perspective change if you did the same?

....

....

....

....

....

In what ways do you find yourself blessed because you have believed that God would do what He said He would do?

....

....

....

....

Anna

LUKE 2:1–40

Anna the prophetess prayed unceasingly, patiently awaiting God's long foretold promises and prophecies to become a reality. How expectant is your faith in what God is going to do in your life and in the world? How might you work to look forward with expectant hope, to linger longer in prayer?

In what ways have you made God the center of your world? What can you do to get back or closer to Him?

Mary, Lazarus' Sister

Mary's sister Martha was worried and upset. Yet Mary herself was calm and determined to sit at Jesus' feet, regardless of what others said or did. What about your life is making you worried and upset? How might these anxieties keep you from choosing the good thing— snuggling close to Jesus, keeping your focus on Him, and listening attentively to what He has to say?

What barriers do you break through to get close to Jesus, to anoint Him with your time and devotion?

Mary Magdalene

—— JOHN 20:1–18 ——

Mary Magdalene would not rest easy until she had found Jesus and done for Him what she could. In what ways do you have Mary Magdalene's determination, love, and patience to seek, serve, and find Jesus?

....
....
....
....
....

In what situations have you felt tired, desperate, confused, uncertain, disconnected, and begun weeping, wondering where Jesus is and how you might find Him?

....
....
....
....
....

How many turnings do you need to take to recognize that the Jesus whom you seek is standing right in front of you, gently and lovingly calling your name?

....
....
....
....

Dorcas and Lydia

Dorcas always helped others. The merchant Lydia offered her heart to God and her home to His servants. What kinds of things do you do for others? How does that "raise you up" spiritually, emotionally, and mentally? How does it delight God—and you?

....

....

....

....

....

What, through prayer and worship, has the Lord opened up your heart to today? How does that move you to open up yourself to others?

....

....

....

....

....

In what ways do you encourage and minister to other believers?

....

....

....

....

....

Priscilla

ACTS 18

Paul met Aquila and his wife Priscilla, both of whom were tentmakers, and began a ministry with them. Who has God brought into your life—a new friend, relative, coworker, fellow believer—with whom you are prompted to begin a ministry? What kind of ministry might that be?

Whom might you feel urged to take aside and explain the way of God more accurately? How might that lead to God's Word being spread even further?

What fellow believer can you encourage today?

30 Days of Bible Readings
on Gratitude

Don't worry about anything; instead, pray about everything.
Tell God what you need, and thank him for all he has done.
Then you will experience God's peace, which exceeds anything we
can understand. His peace will guard your hearts and
minds as you live in Christ Jesus.

PHILIPPIANS 4:6–7 NLT

*I*magine what an amazing world you would live in if you
endeavored not to worry about anything but instead went to
God about everything. Telling Him what you need while thanking
Him for everything He has done. Allowing your needs and gratitude
to shape your prayers as prompted by the Spirit. Not worrying about
getting anything wrong. Knowing the Spirit will make it sound right
to God—the one who knows you like no other being knows you.

Taking on a spirit of gratitude and prayer will help you, even
during the hardest times, to experience that overwhelming and
mysterious peace of God.

Begin here. For the next 30 days, read the Bible passages that
follow. Underline the verse that most touches you. Meditate on
what you've read. Then go to the journaling prompts, asking God
to enlighten you, to tell you what He wants you to hear, know, remember. Then, at some point before you retire for the evening,
write down five things for which you want to thank God, whether
those things be little or great. And soon, you will be overwhelmed
with not only gratefulness but peace in Christ Jesus.

God Is Our Shield

PSALM 28

Which of these cries from the psalmist speaks to you the most? How does that cry compare with what is going on in your life right now? What remedy does this psalm provide you for dealing with whatever issues are before you?

....

....

....

....

....

In what ways does your trusting in God from the bottom of your heart strengthen you spiritually?

....

....

....

....

Imagine God as being your impenetrable shield, your fortress, the shepherd that protects and nourishes you and will carry you forever. Pen a prayer of thankfulness for all He is to you.

....

....

....

....

....

God Hears Us

When have you felt as if you'd been swallowed by a great fish? What steps—thoughts and actions—did *you* take that led you there?

Suffocating seaweed wrapped around his head, leaving him without hearing, breath, or speech, Jonah sank. In what ways do you free yourself of the tentacles that threaten to pull you down and away from God?

When has your mere remembrance of the Lord snatched you from the jaws of death and led you back to life? What praise did you offer to God in response?

God Is Merciful

PSALM 33

God's Word holds true. His plans can never be thwarted. How has that been proved in your life? How does knowing that God's plans cannot be shaken help you make plans?

....

....

....

....

....

How does the unfailing love (aka mercy) of the Lord fill the earth—and you? In what ways do you rely on that unfailing love?

....

....

....

....

....

In what ways does God's loving-kindness help you to wait on and hope in Him? How does it help you extend mercy to others?

....

....

....

....

....

God Is Faithful

How do you continually seek and search for God and His strength? How does doing so lead you into worship?

....

....

....

....

Think about the blessings God has bestowed on His people and on you. How does remembering all the good He has done reinforce the idea that God is faithful to you and His word—and always will be?

....

....

....

....

....

In what ways has God protected you in the past? In the present? How does thinking about God's faithfulness to you increase your faithfulness to Him?

....

....

....

....

....

God Is Accessible

Where do you go when your inner self wants to drink of God, when you are thirsty for Him, His love, His presence?

When was the last time your heart was breaking; your tears were your only food; people were taunting you and your faith; you could barely remember the last time you worshipped God? What did you do for relief?

In what ways can you find God not only when you're on the mountaintop but when you're stuck in the valley?

God Is Good

Ezra 3:7–13

The temple of God is within you. In what ways have you started to rebuild that temple, worked on the structure that houses the Spirit of God? What are you giving, supplying, ordering, and actually doing to gird yourself up?

How and when do you celebrate every completed step of the process? What do you do to praise and thank God?

What song might you write to express all the joy you have in the fact that God is so good—and His love endures forever?

God Provides for Us

PSALM 65

God has many names, one of which is Yahweh-Yireh—God the Provider (Genesis 22:13–14). How does the idea that God will provide all you need help you annihilate thoughts and feelings of lack?

....

....

....

....

How might you thank God for the blessings and joy you receive because He has created *you*, chosen *you*, and craves *you*?

....

....

....

....

In what ways do you find God faithfully answers your prayers in the past and present, giving you hope for the future?

....

....

....

....

....

God Is Praiseworthy

In what ways are your songs of praise and thanksgiving, your expressions of gratefulness, more pleasing to God than an animal sacrifice? How does God grow greater with your praise? How do you grow humbler?

....

....

....

....

God hears all your cries for help. What are you crying out for today? What would you like to praise Him for tomorrow?

....

....

....

....

What do you do to seek God first in your life, requiring Him above all other people, places, and things? How does doing so strengthen your heart and encourage you?

....

....

....

....

God Is Our Salvation

ISAIAH 12

No matter what is happening in your life, God wants you to turn to Him, to bring you home, into His presence, where you belong. In what ways do you crave His comfort and protection today?

How does the idea that God is your source of strength and your song of joy help you to trust Him and have courage?

In what ways do you tell others what God has done in your life? How does your praise spread His fame and name?

God Works on Our Behalf

God has so many different names—Abba, Provider, Creator, Comforter, Shepherd, Healer, Peace, Protector, Friend, Redeemer, Restorer, Rock, Living Water, Lord of Hosts, etc. How do these names help you to remember all the wonders God has performed, is performing, and will perform? Which one speaks the most to you today?

....

....

....

....

....

....

....

What praises come to your lips knowing that God, the one who is on your side, will decide who rises up and who falls? How does that help you to face today and hope in tomorrow?

....

....

....

....

....

....

....

God Restores Us

JEREMIAH 30:18—22

God is continually asking you to "Behold." What is He wanting you to see with eyes of expectation?

....

....

....

What happens when you, from a place that seems beyond repair, begin praising God, knowing He will come to your side and build you up all over again? What is God moving to restore in your life? What praises will you sing as He raises everything?

....

....

....

....

How does it feel knowing that, through thick and thin, ups and downs, God will always be your God and you will always be His daughter?

....

....

....

....

God Is a Great God

What does it feel like when you come into the grandeur of God's presence? What do you see and do? What does He see, hear, and do?

....

....

....

....

God is not only amazingly grand and awe-inspiring as a mountain but also as personable and intimate as a shepherd with you as His precious lamb. In what ways might He be urging you to heed His voice so that you will be safe and secure?

....

....

....

....

....

....

How does your praising God's grandeur help you enter into His rest?

....

....

....

....

....

....

God Mends the Broken

JEREMIAH 33:1–11

God yearns for you to call to Him so that He can answer in wisdom, strength, and healing. How do you call on God?

....

....

....

....

What amazing things, what secrets might the Lord, the One who made heaven and earth, be ready, willing, and waiting to tell you if you would only ask?

....

....

....

....

....

In what ways can God's words heal you, stitch you up, strengthen you, rebuild you? How do you still the chatter in your mind and open the sections of your heart to mentally and spiritually hear God's voice?

....

....

....

....

....

God Cares for Us

You are a sheep in the pasture of a God who gives you continuous and unfailing love. How secure and cared for does that make you feel?

....
....
....
....

How do you enter God's gates? With thanksgiving and praise or resentment and complaints? In what ways might your response be dependent on or tainted by what's going on in your life? How might your praise turn your life around?

....
....
....
....
....

What can you do to make "Thank You!" your password into God's presence?

....
....
....
....
....

God Sees the Big Picture

2 CORINTHIANS 4:7—18

Even when you are pressed on every side, confused, and perhaps even despairing, God, who sees the big picture, has got you covered. He equips you with *His* power, the same power that raised Jesus from the dead and overcomes all things. How might that fact change your perception of helplessness in some situations?

How do you tap into God's renewing power every day? In what ways can you keep your eyes focused on the things that cannot be seen and put your hope in them?

God Is Our Strength

Your God has strength beyond what any human can imagine. How might telling others of God's strength and all He does make you stronger?

....

....

....

....

....

What happens on days when you try to do things in your own strength? What happens on days when you take the time to tap into God's strength? How can you tap into God's strength continuously?

....

....

....

....

....

What words of gratitude come to your mind when you consider all that God has strengthened you to do?

....

....

....

....

....

God Loves Cheerful Giving

2 CORINTHIANS 9:6–15

How can you make what you give to God something that is between Him and you alone, with no word to nor pressure from anyone else?

....

....

....

....

God wants you to give from the heart and will bless you back in accordance to that amount—no more, no less. How might that take the guilt out of your giving—more or less?

....

....

....

....

....

Your giving blesses you, the giver; others, the receivers; and God, the provider. How will you thank God for the threefold blessings of your giving?

....

....

....

....

....

....

God Rescues Us

PSALM 106:1–8

God is your ever-vigilant lifeguard. From what things does He rescue you? Which dangers are of your own making?

....

....

....

In what ways do you try to rescue yourself? What usually happens when you take matters into your own hands instead of giving God room to work?

....

....

....

....

....

What powers does God demonstrate when He rescues you? What steps might you have to take to let go of control and allow God to come in and do what He needs to do? How would your letting go make His life-saving efforts easier?

....

....

....

....

....

....

God Preserves Our History

PSALM 106:9–48

You have been a part of God's story—*History*—from beginning to end. What lessons have you learned from it? How does it help you to grow in your faith?

What is the most important lesson you have learned from a person, story, or verse in the Bible? Who is your favorite Bible character? Why? What has this person taught you about life? About faith? About yourself?

Why might God be preserving your own story? How might you thank Him for doing so?

God Blesses Us

EPHESIANS 1:3–14

Because you are one with Christ, God has blessed you beyond belief! What things might keep you from abiding in Christ and receiving every spiritual blessing that comes with that?

Adopted into God's family, you are now a daughter of God. In fact, He actually picked you out for Himself—before the world or you were made! How does this bless you? How might you bless God?

In what ways can you pass God's blessings on to other people? Who might you bless today?

God Satisfies

PSALM 107:1–32

In what ways does God satisfy your soul's thirst and appetite? How does His Word heal, free, and deliver you?

....

....

....

....

If you cry out to God, He will not only calm the waters and still the waves but bring you into a safe harbor! How has God calmed your storm, stilled your waves, and brought you back into the haven you desired?

....

....

....

....

....

....

Where else, besides God, might you be looking for satisfaction? How might He be calling you back to seek Him alone?

....

....

....

....

....

God Raised Jesus

How often do you pray for enlightenment—spiritual wisdom and insight—so that you might better know God and His plan for you?

....

....

....

Reflect on all the incredible power that God has given you. How does knowing that you have the same power that raised Christ from the dead give you more confidence in and gratitude for God and His plan for your life?

....

....

....

....

....

....

What happens to your worries when you remind yourself that Christ is the most powerful and fulfilling person and presence in your life?

....

....

....

....

God Helps Us

God is continuously looking to lend you a helping hand, to reach into your life and pull you out of potential quagmires. In what areas of your life might you be looking to people instead of God for help? In whom is your confidence?

....

....

....

....

....

Why is it so much better to trust and take refuge in God rather than earthly rulers?

....

....

....

....

How does knowing God will help you and His love for you is forever give you confidence to face anything and everything, no matter who or what is against you?

....

....

....

....

....

God Fights for Us

PSALM 118:13–24

God's right arm has more power than your entire body. How might you be trying to battle things with your own strength? How might you begin to let God fight for you?

....

....

....

....

When has God fought for you in the past? How did it feel to leave everything up to Him, knowing He's got a better plan and the most power?

....

....

....

....

....

What would happen if you looked at today as the day God has given you, and simply rejoice in it, leaving all present and potential skirmishes in God's hands?

....

....

....

....

God Grants Success

PSALM 118:25—29

You can pray for God to give you success. Ever tried it? What stops you from doing so? How might your prosperity in life and spirit actually be a win for God?

....

....

....

....

In what ways does God shine His light into your life, leading you to make better decisions?

....

....

....

....

When has God given you success? To whom did you give the credit? When was the last time you thanked Him for granting you victory? Why might it be better to shine the light of your success on God instead of yourself?

....

....

....

....

....

....

God Brings Peace

God's Word tells you to consistently rejoice in the Lord, no matter what is going on in your life. How can you make rejoicing in God a habit?

How does a continuous conversation with God—telling Him all your needs and thanking Him for all He has already provided, is providing, and will provide—help you recognize and experience His peace?

What are some things you think about or verses you mediate on that can help you keep your mind on praiseworthy things?

God Is Loving

PSALM 138

The psalmist David thanked God with all his heart. What is your praise and thankfulness to God like? Half- or wholehearted? Restrained or free-flowing? Rare or common? Sparse or teeming?

In what ways does your loving God answer you as soon as He hears your prayer? In what ways does the strength He gives encourage you?

God loves you. How does this give you confidence that He will indeed work out all His plans for your life, finishing what He's started in you?

God Makes Us Righteous

To what has God called you? How does He help you to live a life worthy of Him and His purpose for you? How do your prayers help you stay on the right track with God?

....

....

....

God gives you the power to do *all* your faith has prompted you to do. How do you home in on those promptings? How long does it take you to respond?

....

....

....

....

....

How does your right living in accordance with God's will and way honor Him?

....

....

....

....

....

God Heals the Heartbroken

—— PSALM 147 ——

God's main interest is in you, His daughter. He longs to mend you, bind up your wounds, and draw you into His arms, to let you cry upon His shoulder until you are ready to face the world once more. What balms does God provide you?

....

....

....

....

....

When was the last time your heart was broken? In what ways did you seek God's healing touch?

....

....

....

....

....

How does the fact that God is all-powerful and filled with understanding make it easier to run to Him for solace rather than to a fellow human?

....

....

....

....

God Conquers All

Nothing is more powerful, wonderful, or loving than God. How would you describe His power? How would you describe your own? How does this comparison help you to leave your battles in God's hands?

....

....

....

In what way does your singing praises to God bring you victory before the fight begins?

....

....

....

....

In what ways have you witnessed the overcoming power of God's Word at work in the world? How has God's Word helped you meet challenges and win battles in your own life?

....

....

....

....

....

....

30 Days of Bible Readings
on Forgiveness

Clothe yourselves with tenderhearted mercy, kindness, humility, gentleness, and patience. Make allowance for each other's faults, and forgive anyone who offends you. Remember, the Lord forgave you, so you must forgive others.

Colossians 3:12–13 NLT

God's forgiveness! How unbelievable, miraculous, and wonderful is His grace, His unmerited favor, His love and kindness! The more you understand how God has forgiven you, the more you will love Him and find it in your heart to forgive others in your life.

Feelings of bitterness, thoughts of revenge, emotions embedded in frustration, all these things fade away the more you realize exactly what God has done for you through the death of Jesus. And the more humbled you will become as you seek the forgiveness of others, as well as forgive others, including yourself.

Many wonderful things are in store for you in the next 30 days as you gain an understanding of what God has laid out for you in His Word and His plans to help you become what He has envisioned you to be. As always, pray before you read the passage. Underline whatever verse has touched you. Meditate on the scriptures, and then read through, reflect on, and respond to the journal-writing prompts, knowing the Spirit will reveal things you'd never dreamed or imagined.

A Brother Forgives

A deceiver humbled himself, seeking a much-desired forgiveness from the person he'd wronged. Have you ever done the same? How did you garner the courage to approach the person? What precautions did you take? What appeasements did you make?

What prayer might you pray before approaching someone to ask for forgiveness? What promises of God might you keep in mind to bolster your resolve?

How might your feeling unworthy of God's love, faithfulness, and forgiveness help you to extend your love, faithfulness, and forgiveness to others?

The Trespass of Your Brothers

GENESIS 50:1–21

What happens when a mediator—one who was a peacemaker between you and another—is no longer on the scene? How might God's grace help you in your relationship with that other person?

How does the idea that it is God who doles out justice help you to have peace with God, yourself, and your offenders?

God intends all things that happen to you to be for your good. How does that fact help you to look for the good in all events and people?

God, Merciful and Gracious

EXODUS 34

God lavishes His love on you, forgiving and forgetting all the missteps you have made in your walk with Him. What does that knowledge do for you?

....

....

....

....

How would your perspective and attitude change if you daily asked this great and merciful God to travel with you, to display His power, to go ahead of you and drive away all your true enemies?

....

....

....

....

Write down some of the instructions God is giving to you today. Who might He be wanting you to be merciful and gracious to?

....

....

....

....

No God Like You

1 KINGS 8:22–53

No one, no god, is as true to His people as your God. He hears you no matter where you are—and forgives. What fellow human being forgives you no matter what you say or do? Who do you forgive no matter what? What makes such forgiveness possible?

....

....

....

....

....

In what ways do you walk before your incomparable God with your entire heart and soul?

....

....

....

....

....

When you pray, do you praise God, telling Him there is no other God like Him? How might doing so change you?

....

....

....

....

....

The Good Lord Pardons

When you return to God, He returns to you. In what areas of your life do you need to return to Him? What might you need to submit to Him so that you can breathe easier within?

How does your turning to the Lord, reading His Word and obeying Him, make His working in your life more potent and powerful yet easier and more peaceful?

In what ways do you celebrate the forgiveness of God for all your missteps, misdeeds, and mistakes?

Remember, O Lord, Your Mercies

God has shown you compassion from the beginning. What rebellious misdeeds from your youth now make you cringe? What's it like knowing God has forgiven and forgotten them?

How does God's forgiveness of prior missteps help you learn and grow from them? How might your hanging on to them stunt your spiritual growth? What might God want you to forgive yourself for?

How do God's mercies help you to see the path He has laid out in front of you? How is such sight your choice?

Blessed Are the Forgiven

God not only forgives your disobedience, He removes it from sight. Have you ever before thought of yourself as having a record of misdeeds? What joy does the knowledge God has erased it give you?

....

....

....

....

....

Before you even confess things to God, He already knows all about them. What things have you not confessed, even to yourself? How might it feel coming clean to God—and, in turn, yourself—about everything?

....

....

....

....

What advantages do you find in confessing and being forgiven?

....

....

....

....

....

Show Us Mercy

God has a wonderful habit of giving His people a fresh start. How does your finding and holding on to a new beginning require your assurance of God's love?

In what ways do you find yourself going back and repeating similar offenses against yourself, God, and others? How important is God's mercy when you keep slipping the same old way?

What peace and forgiveness may God be trying to speak into your heart if you would only listen?

God Abundantly Pardons

ISAIAH 55

Do you approach God with your ears wide open, ready to hear directions from Him? What if you made it your number one priority to do so?

Do you approach God with your ears wide open, ready to hear directions from Him? What if you made it your number one priority to do so?

As a daughter of God, you have inherited His promise of pouring out His never-ending love upon you. What would your day be like if you kept this idea in the front of your mind?

What do you consider when you realize God's Word goes out, always bears fruit, and accomplishes His will? What words might God be speaking into your life right now?

He Delights in Mercy

—— MICAH 7 ——

Even if you're sitting in the dark, God provides the light. When have you felt down and alone, thinking not one honest and caring person exists on earth? Where did you find hope?

....

....

....

....

....

Do you confidently wait for God, knowing you'll be amazed at what He eventually does, or are you second-guessing Him around every turn, fearful He's forgotten or is tired of you? Which tack serves you *and God* better? Why?

....

....

....

....

How does it make you feel knowing God not only gives you mercy but is delighted to do so?

....

....

....

....

....

Forgive Us Our Debts

God wants a one-on-one, heart-to-heart conversation with you. Where is your secret closet of prayer? How do you feel when entering? When departing? What is its blessing in your life?

How does it change your prayers knowing God knows what you *really* need before you even begin to ask?

Have you first forgiven the debts others owe you before you ask God to forgive what you owe Him? What dissonance comes up in your life when you don't forgive?

Parable of the Unforgiving Servant

Where two or three of Jesus' believers are gathered, He's there too. If you're having trouble forgiving someone from the heart for the 490th time, what might happen if you asked someone to pray with you—not just for the person needing forgiveness but for the strength to do so?

How might you at times be like the forgiving king? Or the unforgiving servant? How does patience play a part? How patient is God with you?

Why must your forgiveness of others be a prerequisite to God forgiving you?

Blood Shed for Remission of Sins

MATTHEW 26:17-29

Jesus shed His blood so God would not only forgive your missteps, but so you could come to God and be reconciled to Him. What thoughts and feelings come up when you consider that truth?

....

....

....

....

....

How might your refusal to forgive someone be like a betrayal to Jesus, a disregard of all He's done for you? Who does God want you to forgive?

....

....

....

....

In what ways do you pour onto others the amazing love Jesus has poured out to you? Who does God want you to love?

....

....

....

....

Authority to Forgive

MARK 2:1–17

How bold is your belief in Jesus' power and ability to heal you and others of diseases *and* forgive sins? How has He rewarded you and others for that boldness?

....

....

....

....

....

Within His heart and Spirit, Jesus knows your self-talk, thoughts, and feelings deep within your own heart and spirit. In what ways do you sense that truth? How might Jesus' total awareness of you make you become more aware of your inner chatter and emotions?

....

....

....

....

In what ways has Jesus called you, as imperfect as you may be, to follow Him?

....

....

....

....

....

Forgive, and Be Forgiven

Who are your enemies? What makes it hard for you to love and forgive them? What change of attitude/perspective might make it easier?

....

....

....

....

Jesus seeks your compassion toward others. Are you ready, willing, and able to do good to those who hate you? To bless those who curse you? To pray for those who misuse you? To allow others to steal from you?

....

....

....

....

....

How well do you practice the spiritual law of getting what you give? How might that help you to forgive, give, not judge, and more?

....

....

....

....

....

A Sinful Woman Forgiven

LUKE 7:36–50

As poor and blemished as this sinful woman was in the eyes of others, she sat at the feet of Jesus, kissed His holy feet, wiped them with her tear-soaked hair, and anointed them with an expensive perfume. Could you do the same? Will you do the same?

....

....

....

....

....

Who might mock you for or protest your worshipping of Jesus that way, doing what you can to love Him, no matter how unusual and humbling your actions?

....

....

....

How has your faith saved you and led you into peace?

....

....

....

....

....

If He Repents, Forgive Him

In what ways, if any, does the story of the Rich Man and Lazarus comfort you? Convict you?

Jesus wants you to forgive your offenders when they apologize—even if they do that seven times a day! What resentments might you be harboring against people who continually do something against you, say they're sorry, and then do the same thing all over again? What would God like you to do to reach across this chasm of unforgiveness? How might doing so give you freedom?

Father, Forgive Them

LUKE 23:26—43

Jesus said, "Father, forgive them, because they don't know what they're doing." When have you looked at what others were doing against you, the acts they were committing, the statements they were making, and said the same thing? How might that have given you some small idea of what Jesus went through and the extent of His forgiveness for all people, including you?

Have you asked Jesus to remember you in heaven in spite of (or because of) your missteps?

Neither Do I Condemn You

JOHN 7:53–8:11

Jesus teaches you not only through the Word but through the events in your life. How are His Word and your life connecting? What lessons are you learning?

....

....

....

....

Where might you go wrong when you compare your good behavior with the not-so-good behavior of others? How do you look when you compare yourself and behavior with Jesus?

....

....

....

....

Who might you—whether mentally or physically—be accusing, badgering, pointing a finger at, in your life? How would Jesus have you respond to and treat that person?

....

....

....

....

That They May Receive Forgiveness

God promises to raise the dead, lavishly love you forever, give you the desires of your heart, forgive and forget all your sins, etc. In the fulfillment of which of His promises does your hope lie?

....

....

....

....

....

In what ways does God's light outshine your own? To what has His light led you?

....

....

....

....

....

God urges you to become the person He designed you to be. In what ways is God protecting you so you can fulfill His vision for your life?

....

....

....

....

Peace with God, Eternal Life

ROMANS 5

In what ways have you felt unable to help yourself, and Christ came in just at the right time to save you? What does that tell you about God, His forgiveness, and His love for you?

....

....

....

....

....

....

The perfect and innocent, the righteous and compassionate Jesus died for you while you were still a sinner, to make you right with God, restoring your eternal life, love, and friendship with your Creator, the maker of your world. What thoughts and feelings arise when you consider that amazing yet undeniable truth?

....

....

....

....

....

....

....

....

....

Forgive and Comfort

2 CORINTHIANS 2:1–11

Those who hurt you really end up hurting themselves more. In what ways has that been proved in your life? How have you not only forgiven but comforted hurting people so as not to discourage them even further?

....

....

....

....

....

How does your faith help you to see beyond what others see, to respond and not react, to reach out and not ignore, to forgive and not resent, to comfort and not cause heartache?

....

....

....

....

How does your forgiving others with Christ's love overcome the evil powers and plans around you?

....

....

....

....

....

Dead in Sin, Alive in Christ

You were once dead in your sins but now as a believer are alive in Christ! How does that amazing fact help you in your perception of pre-Christians?

....

....

....

....

....

Being saved isn't something you've earned but is because of God's grace. How does knowing that help you in extending the gift of your grace to others?

....

....

....

....

....

How has your being forgiven by God brought you closer to His ideal vision of you, renewed you so that you can do what He planned for you to do long ago?

....

....

....

....

Forgiving One Another

EPHESIANS 4:17–32

The Word encourages you to put aside your old nature and put on your new self. In what ways has Christ's presence in your life opened your mind and softened your heart, bringing you ever closer to discovering and becoming who God intended you to be?

....

....

....

....

....

How does allowing the Spirit to make over your thoughts, attitudes, and perspectives help you to forgive others more?

....

....

....

How much do your words cut rather than encourage, spew anger rather than peace, spread bitterness and confusion rather than forgiveness and understanding?

....

....

....

....

....

Reconciled by His Death

Christ is the visible image of God—who then reconciled everything to Him, including you. How does that change your perspective of God? How might it change your perception of yourself?

How assured are you that through Christ's death you are now in God's presence, totally forgiven, able to stand before Him without a mark on you or a blotch on your record? If needed, what can you do to increase that assurance? How will doing so help you trust God more and bolster your faith?

As Christ Forgave You

COLOSSIANS 3:1–17

Now that you've been raised to a new life in Christ, God wants you seeing *His* reality. What might happen if you thought more about things of heaven rather than of earth?

In what ways might you be trying to battle the dark side of life on your own? How would your life be different if you simply clothed yourself with and allowed His peace to rule in your heart? How much less of a struggle against evil and forgiving others might you have?

Mediator of a New Testament

Christ (the beloved), your High Priest, is the mediator between you (the believer) and God (the blessing-maker). How is your conscience lately? Might there be something lingering there, something standing between you and your wholehearted worship of God? What might the Spirit be prompting you to lay at Jesus' feet?

In what ways has Jesus' once-for-all sacrifice, His mediation between you and God, freed you? How has it inspired you? How does it draw you into a place of eternal worship?

Our Great High Priest

What thoughts and feelings come up when you consider Jesus—your High Priest, Savior, Brother, and Friend—sitting at God's right hand in heaven?

....

....

....

....

What has God opened up for you since you began believing in Jesus? In what areas has Christ given you a fresh attitude, perspective, beginning?

....

....

....

....

....

Better things await you, in heaven and on earth. What are you doing to keep your patience tinged with a sense of great expectation as you continue to do what God has called you to?

....

....

....

....

Patience and Prayer

How might patience transform your prayers and your prayers transform your patience? What would happen to both your patience and prayers if you added praise to your heart-to-heart talks with God?

....

....

....

....

What do you need to pray for? Who do you need to pray for? What or who is the Spirit bringing to your mind right now?

....

....

....

....

God hears prayers and comes up with out-of-the-world solutions. How does it energize you knowing that many people—including Bible figures, people just like you—had their prayers answered in miraculous ways?

....

....

....

....

....

Confess Your Sins

Confessing your wrongdoings and wrong-thinkings brings more of the light of God into your life. What might God be prompting you to come clean about today?

How might confessing your sins make it easier for you to forgive or ask forgiveness of others—no matter how long ago or how recent the wrongdoing?

What words of God are challenging your obedience? How does knowing He is truth, love, and light inspire you to put aside your reservations and do what He's prompting you to do?